OF PERIOD
AND PLACE

OF
PERIOD AND
PLACE

by

JOHN ARLOTT

JONATHAN CAPE
THIRTY BEDFORD SQUARE
LONDON

FIRST PUBLISHED, 1944
JONATHAN CAPE LTD. 30 BEDFORD SQUARE, LONDON
AND 91 WELLINGTON STREET WEST, TORONTO

To
MY WIFE
with thanks for my happiness

PRINTED IN GREAT BRITAIN IN THE CITY OF OXFORD
AT THE ALDEN PRESS
PAPER MADE BY JOHN DICKINSON & CO., LTD.
BOUND BY A. W. BAIN & CO., LONDON

TABLE OF CONTENTS

MY thanks are due to George Rostrevor Hamilton and Andrew Young for advice, sympathy, and, even when they did not approve, kindness, and also to the editors of the following periodicals for permission to include in this book poems which first appeared in their pages: *Horizon*, the *Observer*, the *Fortnightly*, the *Spectator*, *Modern Reading*, *Writing Today*, *English* and *Time and Tide*, and to Mr. Edward Sackville-West of the B.B.C., who has included some of them in his broadcast programmes of poetry.

BACK TO THE FAIR

To-night, a cloud-rimmed flowering of the air
Has made a halo round the Autumn Fair,
That teeming, cluttered, music-churning dream
Where shrieking sirens flaunt their plumes of steam:
Crescendo symphony of penny joys
With counterpoint on counterpoint of noise –
The thwack of balls against the ninepin sheet,
The crunch of cinders under shuffled feet,
The power-impelling engine's rhythmic choke,
The bell that answers swaggered mallet's stroke,
The crang of shots that rake the rifle-range,
And chinking undertone of copper change.

The crowd is thickest round the switch-back's race,
With castanetting wheels, the blur of face,
The rushing round the bends to overtop
The heart-arresting, stomach-stealing drop:
There, organ-throned on high, the chip-faced gods
Still give their little, haughty, clockwork nods –
The hurdy-gurdy, steam-pulsed music stammers
With plinking of their rounded metal hammers.

The sparky hissing of the naphtha flares
Still haunts the thoughts of all my Autumn Fairs,
'The Greatest, Finest Fun-Fair In The Land'.
My coppers tightly clenched in sweaty hand,
There's colour here, and only colour counts,
Those red-lipped stallions are my chosen mounts:
To saddle then, with fancied Cossack spring,

And, knees to flanks and hands to reins I cling,
While, breathless, up and down and round and round
My pure-white steed careers in full-stretch bound;
I look around in dizzy horseman's pride
And scorn those earth-bound crowds who do not ride.
The man who nightly serves the roundabout,
A plimsoll-shod and shabby gipsy lout,
In shoddy, wasp-waist, double-breasted coat,
A greasy, near-silk muffler at his throat,
Whose baggy trousers mask a tiger's stride,
Appears like magic at my stirrup's side
And grins and asks me for my 'tuppence, please',
Then swings away with reckless, lounging ease,
And calmly counts his takings as he moves
Unscathed amidst that race of threshing hooves.

THAT FILM – OR ANOTHER
(A Gothic Exercise)

The thick black cloud slides like a hearse,
The slant rain blackens like a curse,
The wind howls like a teething child
Through statued gardens, long run wild:
The house looms ghastly black-and-white,
Thin chimneys stand up straight with fright.
Into the grizzling, streaming night
A single window carves its light;
The room behind that flaring blind
Is heavy, high, oak-panel lined;
The hound is stirring by the grate,
The candle flares in gold-sheathed state;
The great four-poster, carved and steep
Enframes a grey head, pillowed deep;
For all death's glaze upon the face,
The profile holds the stamp of race;
The loose mouth droops in lines of pain –
A dying Aubrey Smith again.

INVITATION TO THE LOCAL

Swing-doors, dark-curtained, will let you in
To the heat and light and merging din
Of laughter sprung from broad-based humour,
And gossip out of slight-based rumour,
Then weighted pause for the point of a joke
Till sudden roars ride the waves of smoke
To drown the whisper of racing tips
And crackle of bags of potato-chips.

Old women with Guinness and beaver coats,
Scrub-wrinkled fingers and beads at their throats,
Tap gently with tired, black-booted feet
To faded piano's nostalgic beat.

Catch the reflection of beer-engine's brass
In the wealthy brown of a full pint-glass,
Haunting and sad is the smell of spilt beer,
If beer is best, then what heaven is here.

The barmaid twists in her tight satin frock
To look at the pale-faced, oracle clock;
Then shouts and jostling for the night's last drink,
The till-bell rings and the glasses clink.

Now shuffle of boots on the splintery floor,
Warm-breathing crush in the wide-open door,
And the night-wind strikes with cheek-chilling stroke
To carve a deep cleft in the banks of smoke —
They're turning them out at the old 'Black Bull'
For both the till and its fillers are full.

THE OTHER FEAR

Awake and tense in my island bed,
I heard our night-planes overhead,
Felt their growing roaring hurled
To flood my little curtained world,
And, once again, in plane-racked night
Fear hung for me in sound of flight.
Not now the fear of pain and death
To make me check my trembling breath,
But guilty fear for friends who fly,
Simply to do a job or die.

Youth heard the challenge of its times,
And, blind to statesmen's tricks and crimes,
Youth went, to high adventure thrilling,
Not pausing now to weigh the killing –
Flying and fighting in our name –
If blame there be, we share that blame –
Blame not purged by praise of nations
But only by those generations
Who, not needing passports, fly
Unchallenged over common sky.

APRIL, 1944

A pity of rain, in shafts
With clear and high-lined edges
Is ghosting, tower-high,
To hide, then show, the hedges
That, stubby, knotted, run
Above the blackening soil
Scratch-marked for hopeful seed,
Manured with drugging toil.

The lurching crab-tree leans
Across the growth-green gate:
The earth is cracked too deep,
The rain has come too late.

TO ANDREW YOUNG

ON READING HIS POEMS

Behind these limpid words I find
Reflections, in a crystal mind,
Of images so sharp and clear
That I can almost see and hear
The subjects of your calm delight.
The spider-webs of which you write
Are not more accurate, more fine,
More integral, more light of line,
Nor spun by wisdom more innate
Than are these lines where you create
With living eye, with living hand,
Your real and visionary land:
So clear you see these timeless things
That, like a bird, the vision sings.

A SECOND-HAND BOOKSHOP

The sunlight filters through the panes
Of book-shop windows, pockmarked grey
By years of grimy city rains,
And falls in mild, dust-laden ray
Across the stock, in shelf and stack,
Of this old bookshop-man who brought,
To a shabby shop in a cul-de-sac,
Three hundred years of print and thought.

Like a cloak hangs the bookshop smell,
Soothing, unique and reminding:
The book-collector knows its spell,
Subtle hints of books and binding –
In the fine, black bookshop dust
Paper, printer's-ink and leather,
Binder's-glue and paper-rust
And time, all mixed together.

'Blake's Poems, Sir – ah, yes, I know,
Bohn did it in the old black binding,
In '83.' Then shuffles slow
To scan his shelves, intent on finding
This book of songs he has not heard,
With that deaf searcher's hopeful frown
Who knows the nightingale a bird
With feathers grey and reddish-brown.

ON A GREAT BATSMAN

As the gull conceals in easeful glide
The inborn gift to curb and ride
The gale – merging the sea-wind's force
With lovely movement on a chosen course,
So, in timed swoop, he moves to charm
The ball down-swirling from the bowler's arm
Along some glissade of his own creation,
Beyond the figures' black and white rotation.
    Recorded centuries leave no trace
    On memory of that timeless grace.

BRIGHTON

All-electric, down from London,
Every hour the green trains run,
Bearing tribes of worshippers
To the doubtful Brighton sun,

Postcards of the Sussex Downs,
Ice-rinks, music-halls and beer,
Dance-halls, snack-bars and the rain
On the domed and garnished pier.

There's an elegant Adam fireplace
In a third-rate dancing-club,
Forgotten print of the Regent
In a dusty, smoke-fumed pub,

Regency houses, row on row,
In crescent, square and street,
With pediment, pillar and portico,
'BED AND BREAKFAST' all complete.

Strange-wrought Gothic street-lamps,
Churches a-gleam with tile
Jostle the chrome and marble
Of super-cinema style.

From the tomb-like cold Pavilion,
Drawing-Rooms and Dome
Regency ghosts are sweeping
Through the town that was their home.

Do they see the plaster peeling?
The fly-blown fluted ceiling?
Regency houses tumbled down?
Hove another, *nicer* town?
The Phaeton gone for the family car?
Electric light in the Oyster Bar?
And buses bluing the salt sea air
Under the trees in Castle Square?

And would they return to Hell by way
Of Brighton beach on a summer day,
Would they trip with trippers up-to-date,
And, Regency ghosts immaculate,
Arm-in-arm and devil-may-care,
Past the whelk-stalls and through the profanity,
Step down the steep stone stair
Into this huddle of hot humanity?

MORNING PRAYERS

Sullen, separate, down the stairs
To the cold, dark, waiting chairs
Set in rows for morning prayers
The family came.

Papered wall, a floral stream
Dims in tea-urn's wreathing steam,
Lit by struggling yellow gleam
Of gas-jet's flame.

Tired and silent in hindmost row,
Meek domestics kneeling low,
Tight-tied hair and starch-stiff bow,
Each one the same.

High on the wall, in honoured place,
Devoid of heart, or light, or grace,
Heavily scowls grandfather's face
From gilded frame.

Papa with patriarchal air,
Accosts his God in strident prayer;
For vengeance – 'Strike and do not spare'
Makes urgent claim.

Vengeance on an erring child,
A son defiant, callow, wild,
The son he thrashed, renounced, reviled,
But could not tame.

Who now, the reckless, outcast boy,
Crime his living, vice his toy,
Finds in sin unholy joy,
And knows no shame.

Mother and sister love him well
But dare not break papa's stern spell
Consigning the black-sheep to Hell
Who smirched his name.

.   .   .   .   .

Best-seller of eighteen-fifty-three,
In three-decked uniformity,
It contemplates the brevity
Of literary fame.

ODDMENT SALE IN THE PROVINCES

He bows, the yellow-faced shopwalker,
Frock-coated, bald, affected talker,
And waves me with a large curved hand
To where his black-frocked women stand,
Black-mittened and blue-nosed with cold,
Most pleased to do as they are told.

I hush my tread to white scrubbed board
And walk, awe-stricken, through the hoard
Of pinafores, boas and furbelows,
Collars and stays and woollen hose,
Linens, laces and lush brocades,
Bargains and remnants from four decades.

The household god runs over all;
Ensconced within a wooden ball
The money loosened by the sale
Rattles round a rambling rail
To where the glass-boxed cashier sits
To change the money, file the chits
And catapult back with flick of wrist,
Your change, wrapped up in a paper twist.

Behind the forest of tight-rolled bales
The shopgirls titter and tell their tales,
And don't care what the dividends are
At Mumberley's Fashion Goods Bazaar.

A LITTLE GUIDE TO WINCHESTER

At Winchester the smell of guide-books lies
Across the streets with rich mediaeval names,
And snap-views of the long Cathedral rise
Through alley-ways and leaded window-frames.

The buzzing traffic down the High Street pours
To where the Butter Cross juts out, then stops
By old St. Maurice's half-hidden doors,
And cakes and shirts in mild, unbrazen shops.

See, cycling blithely through the grumbling cars,
A Wykehamist, with brightly banded tie,
And, in the basket on his handlebars,
The biscuits, cakes and books he came to buy.

Now, like a matron, over-jewelled and laced,
The Gothic Guildhall by Sir Gilbert Scott,
And, phoney-Tudor, beam-and-plaster faced,
The jeweller's shop Hostel of God-Begot.

Silk stockings and fur coats and dove-grey gowns
Take tea, crook-fingered, in a Norman keep;
While, as the sun moves round behind the downs,
The quiet clergy court cathedral sleep
In houses calm, where time is but a guest:
These men, who soothe a death or bless a birth,
Should know themselves as truly soothed and blessed
By houses that are stone-spelt peace on earth.

Now, in their harsh-lined parlours, stiffly sit
The bitter spinsters and unfriendly wives,
Who chatter acid as they flickly knit,
And detail spite of other people's lives.

Between the broad-set idling water-mill
And where the bright green buses turn and wait,
King Alfred wears the crown of Wessex still,
And lifts his broadsword to the western gate,
So, in obedience to his statued will,
The little Saxons muster to defend
Their stricken, narrow houses on the hill,
The Hardy-Trollope-Walpole city's end.

CRICKET AT WORCESTER, 1938

Dozing in deck-chair's gentle curve,
Through half-closed eyes I watched the cricket,
Knowing the sporting press would say
'Perks bowled well on a perfect wicket'.

Fierce mid-day sun upon the ground;
Through heat-haze came the hollow sound
Of wary bat on ball, to pound
The devil from it, quell its bound.

Sunburned fieldsmen, flannelled cream,
Looked, though urgent, scarce alive,
Swooped, like swallows of a dream,
On skimming fly, the hard-hit drive.

Beyond the score-box, through the trees
Gleamed Severn, blue and wide,
Where oarsmen 'feathered' with polished ease
And passed in gentle glide.

The back-cloth, setting off the setting,
Peter's cathedral soared,
Rich of shade and fine of fretting
Like cut and painted board.

To the cathedral, close for shelter,
Huddled houses, bent and slim,
Some tall, some short, all helter-skelter,
Like a sky-line drawn for Grimm.

This the fanciful engraver might
In his creative dream have seen,
Here, framed by summer's glaring light,
Grey stone, majestic over green.

Closer, the bowler's arm swept down,
The ball swung, swerved and darted,
Stump and bail flashed and flew;
The batsman pensively departed.

Like rattle of dry seeds in pods
The warm crowd faintly clapped,
The boys who came to watch their gods,
The tired old men who napped.

The members sat in their strong deck-chairs
And sometimes glanced at the play,
They smoked and talked of stocks and shares,
And the bar stayed open all day.

MUSIC HALL
(for M. Willson Disher)

Tobacco-smoke is heavy stealing
To the dim, baroque curved ceiling,
Slashed by sword of spotlight beam,
Shot by fiddles' quickening scream.

Decorous, dark-clad, archly bland,
With wink, or twist of head or hand,
The master points his well-worn tale;
The theme is old, its new guise frail,
But it comes from the basic-slag of life
Of lodger, or debtor, or faithless wife,
And the satisfied laughter surges back
As he deftly shifts to another tack
And sings in voice unstrained and strong
An age-old sentimental song:
Two encores, then the curtain-calls
And the star is gone, the tension falls.

As the acrobats twist and turn and soar
The circle-bar fills up once more,
Where Hilda, the barmaid, ash-blonde and tall,
Chaffs with 'commercials' from Rawtenstall,
And adjusts her curls with a petulant twist
That jangles her bangles from elbow to wrist.

They play 'The King', the curtain's down,
The crowds drift out to the harsh, grey town,
To the sudden chill and the yellow light,

The bustle and noise of the city night,
The clang of trams and the horns of cars
As they make their way to the down-town bars,
Warmed to a satisfied, jovial glow
By the gay, unsubtle variety show.

The great hall, naked-lamp-lit, bare,
Doors wide, breathes in the cool night air.

JOHN PIPER'S 'KEMP TOWN'

Above the tarmac's oafish grey,
Rail-hemmed gown aloof drawn tight,
Holding all the summer's light
Regency terrace sweeps away:
Canopied copper-green-bright,
Windows cupping cool reflection,
Moving in the curve of flight.
Nash's visioned warm perfection,
Dream that mocked his cool design,
– Caught in colour, held in line.

MARINE PARADE HOTEL

Fantastic as Fonthill, yet crudely staid,
It bulks like a cloud on the Esplanade:
Gothic-mad architect's crazy trick
Worked in public-convenience brick.
Against the pavement, so greyly prosaic,
It flaunts its name in pink and white mosaic:
The steps are bath-bricked far too white,
The hand-rails burnished far too bright:
The tall walls echo the lightest tread,
The noise-shamed walker averts his head.

The manager, pigeon-holed and sly,
Watches his narrow world go by,
Knows each numbered impersonal door
On each monotonous self-same floor
Hides the betrayal, the secret dirt,
Innocent-seeming, yet selfish hurt:
How under conventional cheap veneer
Of pomp, or hearty tweeds-and-beer
Are false-teeth, wigs and too-bright dyes,
The corsets, the pads, the drops-for-eyes –
Shams to make the shams respectable.
Never suspecting their tricks detectable,
Daily they move in ghoulish charade
Across the pseudo-Baroque façade.

From 'Tudor' bar and beer swill-tainted,
Walls and women bogus and painted,
At half-past-ten I must stagger away

As they count the cash of a well-spent day,
Into the sea-front's wind-crammed night,
Where, from squat windows, curtained tight,
The narrow jets of light escape
To fall across the road like tape.

There are quiet women in the shadows, waiting,
A smell of cabbage rising from the grating;
No, the people scuffling at the refuse-bin
Do not consider they are 'living in'.

SOUTHAMPTON

The ocean liners' towering funnels
Looming over the gaunt, bent cranes
Merge with the town like painted turrets
Springing from the dock-side lanes.

Galleon tram-cars gong and rattle
Round the Bargate to the Quay
And the unexpected glimpses
Of a grey, unsea-like sea.

On the wharves each blear-eyed warehouse
Blunts the tang of sailors' tales:
Strictly business: care with cargoes:
Scour the cabins: stow the mails.

Come cruising from 'The Ocean's Gateway',
Will you go White Star or Red?
Dancing, cocktails, Tourist Class,
Put to sea on a feather-bed.

There are elms along The Avenue
Where General Gordon rode,
And milk-bottles daily broken
On Honeysuckle Road.

LONDON APARTMENT, 1899

The sleek, black velvet curtains strike
Like sin against the scarlet wall,
And writhe each time the window-breeze
Disturbs their morbid, slinky fall.

In gentle spirals, silver smoke
Is rising from a tube of jet
That holds, in long and languid line,
A hashish-tainted cigarette.
The nervous hand that palely droops
Below the cushions' wine-stained silk,
Now moves to stroke the sugared glass,
Absinthe, as smoky-white as milk.

There, on the lacquered table-top,
An onyx sphinx, with ruby eyes,
Calls back her age-long, baffling gaze
To contemplate, with mild surprise,
The Beardsley drawing on the wall —
A pallid girl, who cowers down
And bleeds as whip-strokes flay her back
To rip the skin-tight, curving gown
In strips that, falling round her feet,
Are merged, with flourish of design,
Among the stinging, arch-black strokes
Continuing the whip-lash line.

The quartered years of Yellow Book
Are neighboured by the latest play

By Oscar, verse by Wratislaw,
By Dowson, Davidson and Gray,
And all their slim and fine-bound kind –
The writings of an age that bred,
In desperate, gaslit wickedness,
The precious heirs of Bodley Head.

The dressing-gown is thrown aside –
A careless twist to flowing tie,
A dash of scent, a catlike yawn,
The drops to kindle bloodshot eye,
A brandy to attune the heart,
The hair swept back with trembling hand,
Then down the stair in curve of cloak
To hail a hansom in the Strand.

In half-light at the Cheshire Cheese
To-night, the Rhymers' Club will dine,
To-night a decade toasts decay,
With myrrh and aloes in its wine.

THE OPENING OF THE GREAT EXHIBITION
1851

(a halfpenny broadsheet to be sold in the grounds of
the Crystal Palace)

Beneath John Paxton's domes of glass,
The crowds get up from dew-drenched grass
Where they have slept all through the night,
For now, through clouds, the sun shines bright,
And glass walls wink its brightness back.
Now, stepping sternly down the track,
The Duke of Wellington is here,
Be-spurred, be-medalled and severe:
He spoke the riddle-solving words[1]
That brought the hawks that killed the birds
That sullied *Queen Victoria's* hat
From early nests on which they sat
In Sibthorp's elm, historic tree,
That emblem of democracy –
Despite a Royal Prince's will,
The people's tree is standing still.

But now, a carriage draws in sight,
The Empire's sun puts forth more light –
Fire cannon now, in loud report –
  Shout HURRAH! HURRAH!
  Here's *Queen Victoria*
  And Albert, Her Consort.

---

[1] 'Sparrow-hawks, ma'am.'

SLUM

(A touch of Gissing)

The stucco peeling from the walls
Dissolves, in smoke-drenched grass,
With chips of chimney-pots and tiles
And broken window-glass.

Inside, the crumbling plaster grates
More harshly on the stair
And rises in an angry cloud
On warm, bug-tainted air.

He is at home, as always now,
And, once again, asleep
On that chair-bedstead by the wall
In hot, untidy heap.

A waste of slates reflects the sun
Back through the window pane
To light the spectrum into life
In every oily stain.

The gas-globe hangs from slender stem,
A fly-blown sickly bloom
That chatters in its copper ring
At each step in the room.

The sleeper wriggles in his sleep,
The bed-slats groan and creak,
The loosened spittle at his lips

Is stretched across his cheek,
And one hand moves up to his chest,
The hairy fingers slowly splay
And grope, as if to scratch the itch
Of lice and life away.

SOUTHAMPTON WATER

The fog is lying, grey
As sorrow, on the tide
That clears the half-sunk buoy
In sulky, humping stride,
And sucks at shingle-banks
With fierce, eternal greed.
Beyond this grey-walled world
Of water, pier and weed,
With saddened foghorn cry,
An unseen ocean-tramp
Is trudging back to sea:
Her pistons' dogged stamp
And water-churning rush
Are filtered echo-thin.
Now, through the wall of fog,
The steamer's wash sweeps in,
A huge and crested wave
With writhing undertow
Of dimpled strength, to strike
With sudden, cunning blow,
The dinghy at the pier,
And then, in tumbling ride,
To climb the drying beach,
Reverse the ebbing tide.
Behind its grim retreat
In shingle-grinding boil,
It leaves the groaning stones
A rainbow coat of oil.

The fog-banks gently hold
The foghorn's dying wail
And, in their shapes, recall
A whispered ghost-ship tale.

TEA WITH MY AUNTS

Tea with my aunts at half-past four,
Tea in a world without a war;
The Widow-Queen is still alive
In grandpa's house in Albert Drive,
And firm the monkey-puzzle tree
He planted at the Jubilee.

A frilly, fragile cup of tea
Unsafely balanced on my knee,
Aunt Anna mellows as I take
Another slice of home-made cake,
She rustles in her stiff grey gown
And takes her endless knitting down.

A chastely-ringed and blue-veined hand,
A weak white neck in velvet band,
With modest touch Aunt Susan plays
The tranquil 'Sheep May Safely Graze'
Of Bach, the tune she used to play,
On Sunday evenings years away,
To whiskered men of gentle sort
Who paid her strained and stately court.

The Landseer cattle on the wall,
The massy antlers in the hall,
The monumental two-year clock,
A faith in class as firm as rock,
And all the house, are just the same
As on the day the family came,

Firm barred against the new and strange
And devil-prompted thoughts of change.

Those gilt-edged shares will never drop,
But yearly yield a steady crop
To feed a world of certain grace
Where servants know their proper place.
The bombs that broke the windows here
Have not disturbed the atmosphere.

ISLE OF WIGHT

When the English found this island
They publicized its charms,
And camped on it and tramped on it
And picnicked on its farms.

The paddle-boats brought the trippers
To the half-mile pier at Ryde
In linen slacks and aertex shirts,
Their women at their side.

The folk of the doll's-house island
Found the invaders strange,
And hid in their little houses,
Out of speaking range.

To the check-square fields came the holiday-camps,
Speed-boats to the river,
The twisting roads were dinned and thronged
By bus and bike and 'flivver'.

To the garden-isle came the tourist trade,
The Needles an afternoon trip,
'Five bob all round the Island'
In a snorting little ship.

But the first hard frost of winter
Sends the hiker to his den,
The islanders come, through unbolted doors,
Into their own again.

The foreigners' cars are ferried away,
The narrow roads are clear,
And island men in island pubs
Quaff mugs of island beer.

In the quiet night they saunter home
To sure, untroubled sleep:
They linger to talk at street corners,
In voices unhurried and deep.

THE OLD CRICKETER

He sits alone to watch the men
At cricket on the village green,
And savours calmly, once again,
The life-remembered, quiet scene
That to his ageing sight grows dim,
And then he sees, with clearer eye,
That these men's fathers play with him,
Their fathers' fathers standing by.
He leaps once more, with eager spring,
To catch the brief-glimpsed, flying ball
And quickens to its sudden sting:
The brightness dies: the old eyes fall,
They see, but do not understand,
A pursed, rheumatic, useless hand.

PRAYER FOR AN IMMORTAL LINE

Now passes basic metal from my brain,
Slow melting through the deep-banked fires of
thought
For spark-flung forging into lengths of chain,
Each link with hammer, sweat and fervour wrought,
Each link then filed with patient, craftsman care
Until the crude and hard-wrought edges show
The humble metal's native greyness bare,
Then polished grimly to a sullen glow.
Yet, while I work, I know these chains must snap
Beneath the tug of time, and, rusted red,
Will pass, rejected, to the age's scrap.
But yet I pray that, when my name is dead,
One age-proof link will still reflect the light,
Its temper fix the smith's endeavour bright.